Hasan Yahya

The Concept of
Crescentology

In Sociology

@ Hasan Yahya Publishers, USA 2012

مطابع القدس

ضمن مشروع إحياء التراث العربي في المهاجر
بدعم من الموسوعة العربية الأمريكية ومعهد التراث العربي
ومطابع القدس – الولايات المتحدة

ISBN-13: 978-1477680964
ISBN-10: 1477680969

Mental Voyage Series - 20

Manufactured in the United States of America

The Concept of Crescentology

The concept of Crescentology is originated by this author, provided here for the third time after researching the concept for 20 plus years of research on the topic. Educationally, it belongs, however to sociology subject matter. Other related concept came out is "socio-therapy" covered in other publication in the same series.
.

Try to understand this extreme statement:

A and B are two persons disputing: A knocks B down, kills him, and then concludes that he who is alive have been right, and that he who is dead must have been wrong.

and this moderate statement:

Here are two other men (also A and B) disputing: one says to the other,
" Let us not fight—we may both be killed; let us take our difference to some elder of the tribe, and submit to his decision."

The first statement is a conflict mode demonstrated and still accepted in both international and intra-national disputes. It is also accepted in both civilized and uncivilized or in both more developed and less developed countries. The second statement, is a critical moment in human understanding, normalizing relationships and promoting conflict resolution. Depending on the negative answer in the second statement, conflict continued (depending on spiritual or material power), and on the positive answer, civilization may plant another root for solutions for peace. But the question remains for crescentologists to pose and search: What powers direct people toward conflict or peace? In other words: what are the determinants of conflict? This , in fact, constitutes the subject matter of Crescentology. To prepare nations, groups, organizations and individuals toward positive answer in the second statement, Theory C, or Crescentology must be understood and practiced on these grounds.

The concept "Crescentology" is a combination of two words, crescent which means the changing shapes of the moon, and logo which means word. As a term, it means: A word about changing parts. Applying the phenomenon of crescent transformation to culture and society by talking about its transformation (or change) from one stage to another is Crescentology. In other words, it is the scientific study of the cultural perceptions including behavior of small and large organizations. It is the combination © of psychology (as A or B) and sociology (as A or B) sciences in studying social behavior. According to this definition, Crescentology covers both macro and micro levels. Cultures as we know have different perceptions on themselves and others. These perceptions influence the individual and the group social behavior. To illustrate, the ingredients of culture from Individuals to whole nations are brought up to perceive "we" as good, and "they" as bad. Social behavior differs among people according to these perceptions. Crescentology is the study of this phenomenon, "we" as A, and "they" as B. Both perceptions interchangeably are the same. Because "We" for us is "they" for others. And "They" for others is "we" for themselves.

Crescentology and Theory C.

Crescentology is theory C. of conflict management. It is the comparative study of the two perceptions in order to integrate them in one concept "C" which means "(ALL= A + B = C). The concept of Crescentology came from the crescent. When the month starts, the crescent shows one part of itself, and this part grows until it becomes "whole moon". The whole moon is in itself Crescentology which means "the whole picture or the total truth" about what we see. It is neither the crescent at the first half of the month (which can be termed as A), nor the crescent at the second half of the month (which can be termed as B). The minute when the crescent becomes a full moon, then Crescentology is at work. This means, that the truth (as a combination of A and B which is in this regard C) must be known, learned, and distributed for both A and B cultures, societies, organizations, families, groups, and finally, individuals. Theory C., or Crescentology, is a call for introducing a new order of relationships among human beings.

Origins of Crescentology

Origins of Crescentology are of three roots: the metaphysical root, the supernatural root, and the positivistic root.

A. The metaphysical Root:

The letter C. in English has more than one pronunciation. It is sometimes pronounced as "S" or "K", other times it is pronounced as "C" or "CH". It is in this case similar to the changing shape of the Crescent. Some Mysterious words also begin with "C". Like the mystery of "Creation", the shape of "Cosmos" (Universe) as "Circle" with "Core" point as "Center". Furthermore, human life is a "Cycle" or "Circle" where it develops cognitively and physically from weak to strong, and from strong to weak according to chronicle order. And where human beings live in a "City" and "Country", under certain "Constitution" or "Custom". And conform to a "Culture". If they deviate, they will be introduced to a "Court" according to a "Constitution", or to the "Cult" rules for punishment.

These concepts which begin with the letter "C" may seem artifacts, however, Crescentology may not build a strong argument around them linguistically. Therefore, this root will be sacrificed except the "Crescent" concept, for its relevancy to the theory which needs more elaboration.

The Crescent Phenomenon:

The idea of this theory of Crescentology came to my mind from an observation from nature, namely, the "Crescent" . To illustrate, the crescent we see, in fact, is not what we see in terms of the real shape of the full moon. In other words, what we see may be described as sensually discernible, and sensually indiscernible. Because what we see is not what we in fact should see. The disappearing part of the moon exists eventhough it was not observable in the time of observation. Both parts of the Crescent (the observed and not observed parts) is taken to be named Crescentology, or theory C, which is the truth about the crescent as a full circle (moon). The discernible part is contrasted with WE perception about one's own world, (culture, society, group, family, etc.,). The indiscernible part of the moon is contrasted with THEY perception as "OTHERS" different from WE world. If we substitute this logic in terms of A (WE) and B (THEY) society, group, or culture, etc., then "Theory C." or "Crescentology" would be the total perception of both (WE and THEY) combined. Divided by 2, mathematically it will show as follows:

$$A + B = C / 2 \qquad (1)$$

where A, is the discernible part of the Crescent describes perceptions of WE about WE, individuals, groups, organizations, societies, and cultures. (through knowledge or any other socialization tools), B is the indiscernible part of the moon and describes perceptions of WE about OTHERS, (individuals, groups, organizations, societies, and cultures). And C, is the total moon, and describes both diminution of the TRUTH as perceived by WE and THEY about WE and THEY, (Individuals, groups, organizations, societies, and cultures). This image of C, is the total unity of mutual understanding between WE and THEY. (Figures 1 & 2)

In one point of time, (it cannot be determined by human observation), the Crescent shape will be equally divided between discernible and indiscernible parts (figure 2) . If this observation is possible in natural phenomena, it is assumed to be possible in directing human behavior toward reciprocal understanding between groups. In this case the equation becomes:

$$A = B \qquad (2)$$

In fact, our concern here is not the time or the size of each part of the crescent, but, rather, our concern is to contrast between the changing phenomenon in both crescent and society (or any other aggregate of collectivities or individuals. We know that societies may change by time, power, natural and human resources, and technology. This fact have to be acknowledged in terms of the historical facts and imbalance of world power over time, for instance, while society A, develops itself, society B, is also developing itself in more or less rate. Norms, values, and mores of both societies tend to be internalized and institutionalized, and each of them is becoming farther apart from the other in terms of "WE" and "THEY". In the social world, if we can direct both societies toward exchanging knowledge to understand each other, to appreciate the opposite culture, both societies will come to their senses and compromise their conflicts.

B. The Supernatural Origin:

One of the mistakes of social philosophers across history, is that they rarely (if not never) thought of the universe creation in a holistic view. The term "mistake" and "never" implied explanation and justification when it comes to logical reasoning. What I mean here is, that philosophers, and almost all social scientists have taken the view that religious assumptions about God's creation of the universe and human being as false assumptions. This argument, however, supports the opposite side of the philosophers' assumptions as the only source of truth and follows religious doctrines as they found in religious books, especially the books of the Muslims, Christians, and Jews (al-Qur'an, the

Bible, and the Torah). I would strongly support that we should not reject as false, everything that is said in religious books about God even though it cannot be investigated by reason.

Scientific assumptions about human beings, however, were used by social scientists, for example, anthropologists see man according to scanty fossil evidence as a "violent ape, a noble hunter or a cooperative food sharer living in harmony with nature". (US News & World Report, p.52) . Sociologists, too, follow the assumption that man is god, or that society is god, where both assumptions are rejected in this section of supernatural origins of Crescentology (or theory C). In terms of religious books, neither man nor society are gods. For simple reason, depends primarily upon the assumption that God has power and knowledge which cannot be always obtained by man or society where both have limited ability in terms of time and space.

In an article written in the US News & World Report under the title "The First Human" the writer says:
"While this picture of our ancestors 2 million years ago shows a sophisticated animal superbly adapted to its environment it also reveals a nascent human being, a creature taking the first fundamental steps that drove a permanent wedge between its descendants and the rest of the natural world." (P.52)

The writer then proceeded to describe how the brains of ancient generations evolved, and how it acted as

"a vital link between the body and behavior, creating rapidly evolving cultural adaptations such as tools, communication, cooperation and inventiveness that overcome the physical limitations of teeth." (P.52-54)

Believing this development as true, the writer then assumes that:

"Understanding the origins and development of these quintessential human traits provides the KEY to explaining why we are what we are." (P.54)

The writer continues his argument by comparing those ape-like creatures with modern man. He says:

"Yet, like modern humans, they stood upright and spoke. They had feet that could have danced a waltz and hands with the dexterity to repair a pocket watch. And they made one giant leap, unmatched by any other animal on earth before them: They planned ahead." (P.54),

These speculations in fact, are neglecting the factor of religion where the prophets have told their followers about the first creation of Adam and Eve as humans. Denying this fact, is wasting scientists' time and efforts. My argument here is, how can scientists deal with the logic of, WHAT IF, religions' assumptions were proved scientifically to be true in the future?

This is not a call to believe (the truth about a fact) without knowledge or experience, but scientists have to question themselves, what if we utilize our assumptions to be in congruity with religious assumptions (about facts or perceived as facts)? What if whatever discovery will occur in the future about the origins of our ancestors is not inconsistent with religious facts. What shall we do? In any case, I assume, it will not harm science to investigate scientifically such assumptions for their face value. Anthropologists taking this assumption into account have to broaden their thinking of BEFORE human creation period. While it will take hundreds of years to discover fossils go back to Adam's time. It will take more time to discover fossils of the creation of life BEFORE Adam times. On the same argument, it might take less time by chance or by the help of advanced technology. But their assumptions should be reevaluated and renovated. It would be easier to look at the human creation as one stage in the creation of the universe. While religious people especially followers of Christianity, Islam, and Judaism, (other religions have similar stories) know from their books that the creation of Adam and Eve was only a stage in many stages of creation. However, in this modern time where scientists (as human beings) are happy of what they think they discovered in the last fifty years, they are-still in the knowledge of the universe-look like a four year's old child who discovered her parent's secret rules to cross the street, or to sleep early or to act in certain way with her sister or brother or neighbor.

While these examples may seem inaccurate to describe scientists and philosophers of the time, they are certainly suffice their purpose in the argument.

These examples were given to compare those children with those thinkers and philosophers who deny and ignore the role of religion assumptions and the information contained in the religious books. There was an old story relevant to this statement says: Once upon a time, there was a stupid maniac lived in a town, he threw a piece of gold in a well and began to cry. People of the village came to help him regain the piece of gold. All the village thinkers and wise men contributed their time, efforts, and energies in the search with no success. Then the stupid maniac laughed and announced that he kept the piece of gold tied in his hand and that he did not throw it in the well in the first place.

Darwin, as well as other social scientists who followed his assumptions about the origin of human beings, and built up on his theories took these assumptions for granted. I am afraid after one or two hundred years, people will discover that all was untrue, as the stupid maniac case in the story. And all social scientists efforts will be wasted for a simple reason, they did not take into consideration the information obtained from religious books and ignore the fact (or perceived fact as true) which says: that man was not an irrational mindless ape-like animal in his first appearance on this earth. My argument here depends on the question: why is it wrong to take into account religious assumptions side by side with assumptions obtained by scientific inquiry? This is in fact, what I am calling for from the point of view of Crescentology. Crescentology looks at the whole universe creation before and after the creation of Adam and Eve. These ideas have their roots in the religious books, which are (perceived by scientists) as not proved scientifically as true or wrong. To support the logic of the above argument, the Islamic belief about human creation will be discussed. More specifically, stages of creation before Adam can be deduced from creationists religious books which I call it the "Universe Creation Theory-UCT". This will be covered in the following chapter.

C. The Positivistic Origin:

Theory C. is a combination of theory and methodology of change. It depends on logic and rational reasoning. To illustrate, past cultural experiences shows that recent development of world culture is directed (even slowly by force or otherwise) toward peaceful approaches concerning international, regional, and national conflict situation under the so called "New World Order". Crescentology as a science of culture (and its inter-and-intra-relationships of its units) is assumed to play a new effective role to understand, to explain, to control and to direct these developments for the purpose of planning future relationships among the socio-cultural units: nations, organizations, groups, and individuals. Such relationships have to be planned and dominated by the guidelines of Crescentology. The prepositions and rules of Crescentology guidelines will be discussed under theoretical framework.

D. Syntheses:

Knowledge of human being-as we all know- is imperfect and determined by time and space factors. While both the supernatural and the metaphysical approaches are not proved scientifically to be untrue or true. They constitute in our argument two categories called A and B. The positivistic approach, however, constitutes the origin of Crescentology or theory C. approach as a combination of the previous two approaches. While both approaches depend on religious emotional (irrational) assumptions, the third approach depends on rational assumptions which are created by human beings according to scientific method (may open for new knowledge which may contradict or support the supernatural and the metaphysical assumptions). If the analogy that human beings inherently have limited physical and intellectual qualities is true, then any decision to provide one's evidence over the other is also limited by the fact of methodology utilization to obtain such evidence keeping in mind the imperfectness of human beings in terms of time and space, physical and mental powers should be taken into consideration dealing with such assumptions.

Crescentology does not deny any of the above approaches. Because it is impossible to think and act without certain real or imagined background religiously or secularly. Instead, Crescentology implies utilizing understanding of the above stages for the purpose of surviving in any conflict management process. Logically, schools of thought cannot be defeated for lack of evidence under religious rules. In conflict resolution, understanding the power of supernatural thinking will stimulate certain solutions which would be difficult-if not impossible-to obtain without cultural knowledge (in the religious realm).

We learned that natural phenomena are constructed with no help or assistant from human beings. We also learned that the secrets behind human belief and action cannot be determined fully. Because persons on this planet have their own individual beliefs and actions. These beliefs and actions remain undirected collectively unless they were united under a spiritual Umbrella. Crescentology takes into consideration that the assumptions that these beliefs and actions can be directed toward peace collectively.

If human beings are directed to act (or behave) in certain way where they become unity under Doctrines of Crescentology belief and action, then the possibility of cultural understanding, appreciation, and compromising is expected to increase, and conflict is expected to be reduced, and peace as a final goal is possible. The argument of this broad assumption takes this shape: any assumption concerning human beings should be manipulated to serve the purpose of leading humanity toward peaceful world. Neglecting supernatural assumptions without proof should not be accepted as true. Because science, as it is known is open to all possibilities, and the supernatural theories-if not superior-are not less than human theories in advocating conflict resolution. Neglecting such assumptions-no doubt-influences the findings about social and cultural phenomena, or at least contribute in its limitations

حول مطبوعات الموسوعة العربية الأمريكية
ومنشورات معهد إحياء التراث العربي في المهاجر
Arab American Encyclopedia-USA - Hasan Yahya

About the author
Dr. Hasan A. Yahya الدكتور حسن عبدالقادر يحيى

Professor, Dr. Hasan A. Yahya is a Jordania American writer originally born in Palestine. He's the author of American Arab Encyclopedia (AAE), the Honorary Committee Member of the Arab & Muslim Writers Union-(A&MWU), the Dean of the Arab writers in North America, an SME Expert , and president of DryahyaTV. He's an Arab American writer, scholar, poet and retired professor of Sociology. He graduated from Michigan State University with 2 Ph.d degrees. He published 150 books plus (105 Arabic and 45 English & Bilingual), and 500 plus articles on sociology, religion, psychology, politics, poetry, and short stories. Philosophically, his writings concern logic, justice and human rights worldwide. Dr. Yahya is the author of best selling book: Crescentologism: The Moon Theory, and Islam Finds its Way, in English, and 28 Arabic Short Stories in Arabic, all on Amazon, Create-space and Kindle. He's of encyclopedic nature in knowledge, an expert on Race Relations, Arab & Islamic cultures. His main interested in Philosophy, Religion, World affairs and global strategic planning for the purpose of justice and human rights. www.dryahyatv.com From his quotes: "No body is perfect, mentally or physically" and "If people loose their dignity, No one may imagine what they are capable of doing to regain it.

ولد في مجدل يابا من أعمال يافا – فلسطين عام 1944. تلقى علومه الابتدائية في مدرسة بديا الأميرية في الضفة الغربية أيام احتوائها ضمن المملكة الأردنية الهاشمية وتخرج في جامعة بيروت حاملاً الإجازة في اللغة العربية وآدابها، ودبلوم التأهيل التربوي من كلية القديس يوسف بلبنان، ودبلوم الدراسات العليا (الماجستير) ودكتوراة في الإدارة التربوية من جامعة ولاية ميشيغان بالولايات المتحدة عام 1988، وشهادة الدكتوراه في علم الاجتماع المقارن من الجامعة نفسها عام 1991. عمل في التدريس والصحافة الأدبية. ومنصرف إلى الكتابة في علوم كثيرة تخص علمي النفس والاجتماع والتنمية البشرية ، ألف ونشر العديد من المقالات والكتب باللغتين العربية والإنجليزية ، وله ست مجموعات قصصية وست كتب للأطفال ، وأربع دواوين شعرية باللغتين أيضا. وهو الآن أستاذ متقاعد في جامعة ولاية ميشيغان. وهو عضو جمعية الكتاب العرب والمسلمين في أمريكا الشمالية ومؤسس الموسوعة العربية الأمريكية في الولايات المتحدة ضمن مشروع إحياء التراث العربي في بلاد المهجر .

مؤلفاته:

Arab American Encyclopedia Publications
منشورات الموسوعة العربية الأمريكية
Dr. Hasan Yahya Books - كتب الدكتور : د. حسن يحيى
كتب (بالعربية والإنجليزية) ، قام بنشرها الدكتور حسن يحيى ضمن مشروعه: إحياء التراث العربي في المهجر ، بالتعاون مع الموسوعة العربية الأمريكية التي أسسها أيضا لهذا الغرض ومعهد البحوث الإدارية ومطابع شركة البركان وتلفزيون الدكتور يحيى في الولايات المتحدة :

The Arab American Encyclopedia Publications:
In English:
1. Moon Flowers: Poems, Tales & Politics
2. Poetry Diwan: Love, Fears & Hopes
3. Crescentology: A Theory Of Conflict Management And Cultural Normalization
4. Crescentologism: The Moon Theory
5. Brief Arab & Muslim Ethics: For Non-Arabic Speakers (Bilingual)

6. The Beast In Me America: Arabic Folklore, Tales, Stories, & Poetry
7. Personality & Stress Management: A New Theory
8. Arab Palestinian & Jews: Sociological Aproach
9. Legal Adultery: Sexuality & World Cultures
10. Crescentologism: The Moon Theory

11. Islam: Finds Its Way
12. 30 Tales From Faraway Land: Middle Eastern
13. Brief Islamic History (bilingual)
14. Jesus Christ Speaks Arabic
15. فن أدبي جديدFan Adabi Jadid (bilingual)
16. Protocols of Zion: Trilingual : Spnaish, English & Arabic
17. Prophets Saga: from Adam to Muhammad
18. Al-Akhlaq al-Islamiyyah (Bilingual)
19. Quotes: Love & Humor (Bilingual)
20. Jesus is Different the Prophets History
21. 50 Short Stories (55 words)-Bilingual
22. The Intruder: Bilingual
23. *Alisha and Other Stories.*
24. 70 Very Short Stories (English)
25. *Short Stories from World Literature (Bilingual)*
26. 65 stories for Children 3-12 , (English)
27. Occupation and Other Stories from World Literature –English
28. 85 Fables & Tales for Children 3 to 12 (English)
29. *Naji al-Ali Art Show.* A Palestinian Artist *Ann Mary Thatcher*
30. Princess Imagination: A New Design Novel (English)
31. Al-Hariri Assemblies (Maqamat al-Hariri (English)
32. Water, Population and Conflict in the Middle East.
33. *Princess Diana Still Alive, A New Novel Design. Ann Mary Thatcher.*
34. *Nietzsche On Christianity*
35. *Bertrand Russell: Roads to Freedom*
36. *The Dangers of the GMS:Slideshow & Presebtation*
37. *Ernest HemingwaySuicide Story*

38. *Brief Management: Theories & Applications.*
39. *I Have the Right to be Angry*
40. *FBI Madness Storm , One Act Play*
41. *Nadia: An Innocent Girl from Cairo, Short Story*
42. *Brain and Mind Psychology*
43. *Banning Islam: Petition of Ignorance*
44. *The Wiseman Spirit Still Dancing:Short Story*
45. *The Oldman and the Mower, Short Story*
46. *Al Imam al Bukhari Research Methods*
47. *Secularism: A Response to Sh. Yusuf al Qaradawi*
48. *Family, Leadersip & Problem Solving Games*
49. *Knowledge & Globalization*
50. *Islam & Muslims in America: Sociological Analysis*
51. *The Science of Socio-Therapy*
52. *Defending Islam, Banning Islam*
53. *Defeating PTSD Epidemics*
54. *New Theory of the Universe: A Macro Philosophical Approach*
55. *The Concept of Crescentology in Sociology*
56. *The Old Man & the Mower, short Story*

57. التعاليم الأخلاقية العربية والإسلامية – باللغتين
58. 28قصة قصيرة بالعربية
59. 55قصة قصيرة للأطفال
60. مناهج البحث العلمي في العلوم الاجتماعية
61. أضواء على الفكر الغربي
62. حالات علاجية لغير القادرين
63. علم الإجتماع التطبيقي
64. حكايات من أمريكا
65. قياسات الذكاء بالعربية
66. نظرية سي القمرية والطبيعة البشرية
67. مقالات في التنميةالإجتماعية
68. ديوان بحر الأماني – شعر
69. ديوان القدر – شعر
70. ديوان لولاك – شعر
71. زوجة السلطان -مجموعة قصصية

142. أرض البرتقال الحزين لغسان كنفاني
143. الدفلى: رواية بالعربية لماري رشو
144. الطوفان الأزرق : رواية من الخيال العلمي للكاتب المغربي : أحمد عبدالسلام البقالي
145. في مهب الريح: رواية للكاتب الأردني تيسير دبابنة

أما مقالاته فتزيد على الخمسمائة مقال باللغتين العربية والإنجليزية وهي منشورة على الإنترنت ، وتم جمع بعضها في كتبه الإنجليزية والعربية كل في مجاله .

www.ingramcontent.com/pod-product-compliance
Lightning Source LLC
Chambersburg PA
CBHW070123010626
45794CB00012B/1248